GRAPHIC HISTORY

LORDS OF THE SEA

THE VIKINGS EXPLORE THE NORTH ATLANTIC

by Allison Lassieur
illustrated by Ron Frenz
and Charles Barnett

Consultant:
Roland Thorstensson
Professor of Scandinavian Studies and Swedish
Gustavus Adolphus College
St Peter, Minnesota

www.raintreepublishers.co.uk
Visit our website to find out
more information about
Raintree books.

To order:
☏ Phone 0845 6044371
🖷 Fax +44 (0) 1865 312263
🖳 Email myorders@capstonepub.co.uk

Customers from outside the UK please telephone +44 1865 312262

Raintree is an imprint of Capstone Global Library Limited, a company incorporated in England
and Wales having its registered office at 7 Pilgrim Street, London, EC4V 6LB – Registered
company number: 6695582

"Raintree" is a registered trademark of Pearson Education Limited, under licence
to Capstone Global Library Limited

Art & Editorial Direction: Jason Knudson & Blake A. Hoena
Designer: Jason Knudson
Colourist: Benjamin Hunzeker
Editor: Christopher Harbo
UK Editor: Vaarunika Dharmapala
Originated by Capstone Global Library Ltd
Printed and bound in China by South China Printing Company Ltd

ISBN 978 1 406214 35 2 (hardback)
14 13 12 11 10
10 9 8 7 6 5 4 3 2 1

British Library Cataloguing in Publication Data
A full catalogue record for this book is available from the British Library.

Disclaimer
All the Internet addresses (URLs) given in this book were valid at the time of going to press.
However, due to the dynamic nature of the Internet, some addresses may have changed, or sites
may have changed or ceased to exist since publication. While the author and publishers regret any
inconvenience this may cause readers, no responsibility for any such changes can be accepted by
either the author or the publishers.

CONTENTS

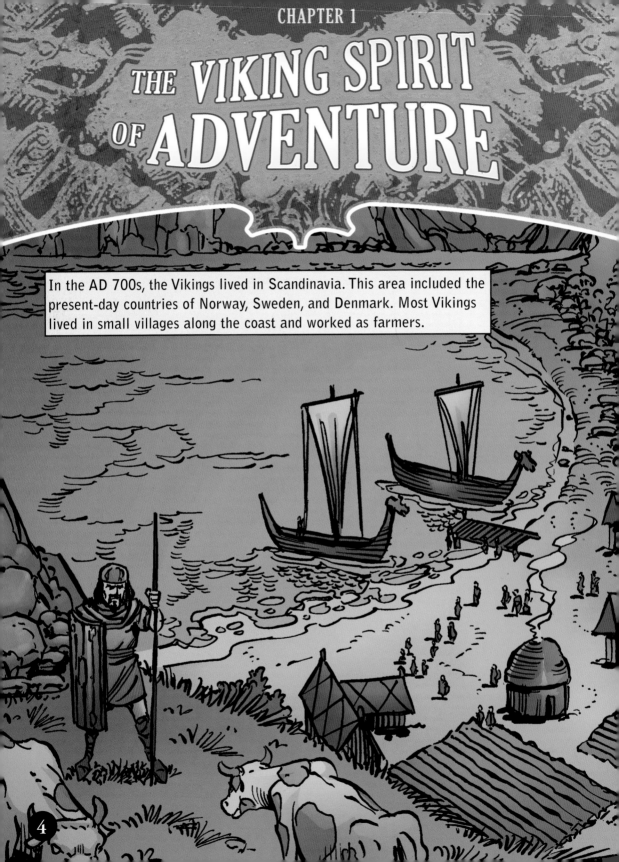

CHAPTER 1
THE VIKING SPIRIT OF ADVENTURE

In the AD 700s, the Vikings lived in Scandinavia. This area included the present-day countries of Norway, Sweden, and Denmark. Most Vikings lived in small villages along the coast and worked as farmers.

The Vikings used rivers and waterways called fjords to travel from village to village. They built strong, fast ships and became excellent seafarers and navigators.

Good farmland was hard to find in Scandinavia. Some Vikings began raiding other lands for riches.

In 793, Vikings landed in England and raided the Lindisfarne monastery.

Search the church! Look for jewels and gold!

Where are you taking me?! Let me go!

You're a slave now! Get on board!

CHAPTER 2

EXPLORING THE NORTH ATLANTIC

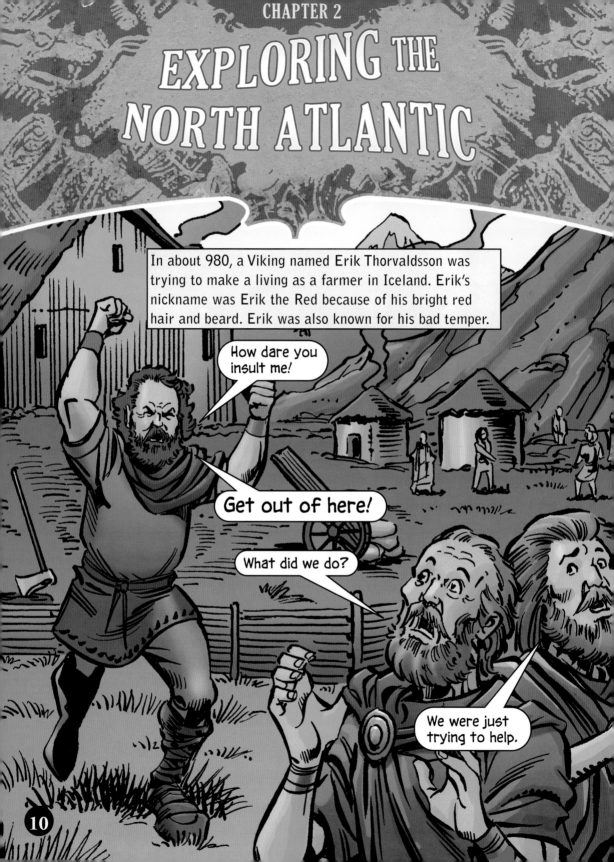

In about 980, a Viking named Erik Thorvaldsson was trying to make a living as a farmer in Iceland. Erik's nickname was Erik the Red because of his bright red hair and beard. Erik was also known for his bad temper.

How dare you insult me!

Get out of here!

What did we do?

We were just trying to help.

In 982, Erik killed two men and was banished from Iceland.

You cannot return for three years!

I've heard there's land to the west. I'll go there!

Erik put together a crew and sailed west.

The stories were true!

The cliffs rise straight out of the sea!

Find a place to go ashore. Let's explore this land.

11

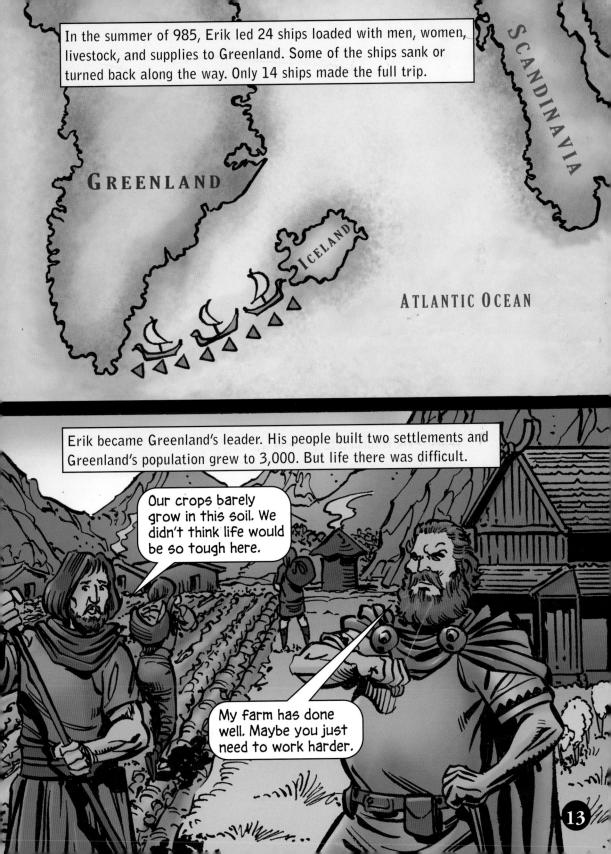

In the summer of 985, Erik led 24 ships loaded with men, women, livestock, and supplies to Greenland. Some of the ships sank or turned back along the way. Only 14 ships made the full trip.

SCANDINAVIA

GREENLAND

ICELAND

ATLANTIC OCEAN

Erik became Greenland's leader. His people built two settlements and Greenland's population grew to 3,000. But life there was difficult.

Our crops barely grow in this soil. We didn't think life would be so tough here.

My farm has done well. Maybe you just need to work harder.

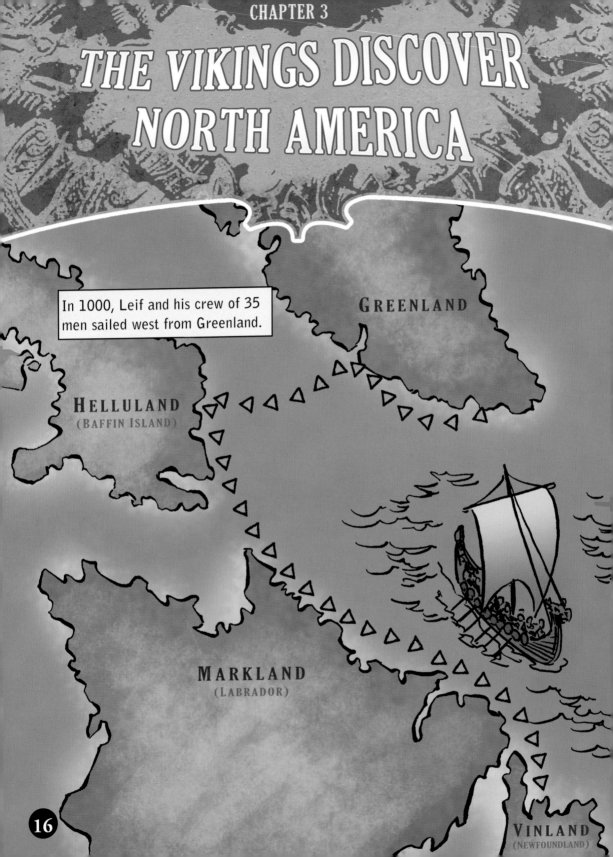

CHAPTER 3

THE VIKINGS DISCOVER NORTH AMERICA

In 1000, Leif and his crew of 35 men sailed west from Greenland.

GREENLAND

HELLULAND
(BAFFIN ISLAND)

MARKLAND
(LABRADOR)

VINLAND
(NEWFOUNDLAND)

While out exploring, they discovered the natural riches of the land.

Leif, look at these vines! They are loaded with grapes!

This is the richest land I've ever seen! I will call it Vinland.

When spring came, Leif and his crew loaded their ship with wood, grapes, and plants and sailed back to Greenland.

Everyone at home will be very excited to see what we've found here.

Sure enough, the Inuit returned in larger numbers and attacked the Vikings.

Thorvald's been hit by an arrow!

He's dead!

After the battle, the crew buried Thorvald near their camp. Then they loaded their ship with wood and grapes and sailed back to Greenland.

23

CHAPTER 4

THE LAST VIKINGS IN NORTH AMERICA

The Vikings made another attempt to settle North America. In about 1020, Thorfinn Karlsefni and 140 other men and women sailed there with supplies.

Will we have enough food and livestock to start our colony, Thorfinn?

More than enough, Gudrid. Our farms will succeed in Vinland.

Unfortunately, Thorfinn's good fortune in Vinland didn't last. After three years, problems began to arise within the settlement.

The winters are too harsh. We should go home.

There are too many men here and not enough women.

The Inuit are angry because we won't trade our weapons with them.

We can make this settlement work!

Finally, trade with the Inuit broke down, and they attacked the Viking settlement.

Our iron weapons are much better than bows and spears!

Yes, but they do us no good if we can't get close enough to use them.

Soon after the battle, the Vikings decided they'd had enough. They packed up their belongings and left Vinland.

After Thorfinn left, very few Vikings ventured back to North America and none of them tried to settle down there.

The Viking settlements in Greenland eventually died out. In England, the Vikings married local people and adopted local customs. In Iceland, they continued to prosper. Today, many Icelanders are related to the Vikings who first settled there.

27

MORE ABOUT
THE VIKINGS

- Vikings are often shown wearing horned helmets, but in reality, their helmets did not have horns.

- Many Vikings had descriptive names, such as Harald Fair-Hair, Svein Forkbeard, and Harald Bluetooth.

- Three days of the week are named after Viking gods. Wednesday is named for the ruler of the gods, Odin. Thursday is named for the god of thunder, Thor. Friday is named after Freya, the goddess of love.

- Around 1500, the Viking settlements in Greenland died out. No one knows exactly why. The Vikings may have died of disease or used up all the natural resources.

- In the 1960s, archaeologists found the remains of a Viking settlement at L'Anse aux Meadows in Newfoundland, Canada. This site is the only known Viking settlement in North America.

The Vikings also travelled east to Russia and the Middle East. Along the way, they traded goods, weapons, and silver with the people they met. They used the silver to make jewellery. Both men and women wore silver rings, necklaces, and brooches.

Vikings travelled on land using horses, wagons, skis, and sledges. They even made ice skates out of animal bones.

The Vikings used a type of ship called a *drakkar* to raid other lands. This ships was also known as a "dragon ship" because of the dragon carved on its front. *Drakkars*, like all Viking ships, were built to travel fast.

The Vikings created the earliest form of parliamentary government in Europe. Known as the Althing, this outdoor meeting allowed free men to voice problems and discuss laws.

GLOSSARY

banish send someone away from a place and order them not to return

colony area that has been settled by people from another country

fjord long, narrow inlet of ocean between high cliffs

Inuit native people of northern Canada, parts of Greenland, and Alaska

navigator person who uses maps, compasses, and the stars to guide a ship

INTERNET SITES

http://www.nmm.ac.uk/explore/sea-and-ships/facts/ships-and-seafarers/the-vikings

You can find out about different types of Viking ships on this website, as well as navigation and life on board the boats.

http:www.historyofyork.org.uk/themes/life-in-viking-york

This website tells you all about when the Vikings captured York.

http://www.bbc.co.uk/schools/vikings

On this website, you can find out about the daily lives of the Vikings, their beliefs, and their settlements.

READ MORE

History of Britain: The Saxons and Vikings, Jane Shuter
(Heinemann Library, 2007)

History Opens Windows: The Vikings, Jane Shuter
(Heinemann Library, 2008)

Men, Women, and Children: In Viking Times, Colin Hynson
(Wayland, 2009)

*New Explore History: Romans, Anglo-Saxons, and Vikings
in Britain* (Heinemann Library, 2005)

BIBLIOGRAPHY

The Viking Saga, Peter Ludwig Brent (Weidenfeld and
Nicolson, 1975)

A History of the Vikings, Gwyn Jones (Oxford University
Press, 2001)

The Vikings, Else Roesdahl, translated by Susan M.
Margeson and Kirsten Williams (Penguin, 1998)

The Oxford Illustrated History of the Vikings, P. H. Sawyer
(Oxford University Press, 1997)

INDEX